# A Trip to Fossil Beach

## By Carmel Reilly

Gavin and his family were going to Fossil Beach to see dolphins.

"Grab your denim jacket, Gavin!"
said Dad.
"It is cold at Fossil Beach."

The family set off.

Gavin was warm in his
denim jacket, so he nodded off.

Robin rolled the window down.

BANG!

Gavin woke with a jolt!

'What was that?" said Gavin.

"A car ran into us!" said Mum.

They all got out of the car.

"I'm so sorry!" said the man
from the other car.
"I made a mistake!"

"It's just a smashed light," said Dad.

Car Help promised to come soon,"
said Mum.
"Let's wait there."

"I'm hungry!" said Gavin.

Dad got the food bag.

"We have some crackers and red lentil dip," he said.

"Yum," said Gavin.

Gavin, Mum, Dad and Robin
sat on a picnic rug playing cards.

Then a man from Car Help came.

"You must be the family with the smashed light!" he said. "I can fix that!"

The man took the smashed light off the car.

He let Gavin help put the new light on.

"You did well!" said the man to Gavin.

When the light was fixed,
the family packed up.

"Have we missed the dolphins?"
said Gavin.

"Yes, it's too late," said Mum.

But we had a great family picnic!"
said Robin.

'And I want to fix cars
when I grow up!" said Gavin.

# CHECKING FOR MEANING

1. Why was the family going to Fossil Beach? *(Literal)*

2. What woke Gavin up? *(Literal)*

3. What did the man mean when he said Gavin did well? *(Inferential)*

# EXTENDING VOCABULARY

| | |
|---|---|
| **denim** | What is *denim*? Do you have a denim jacket or pants? What colour are they? How does denim feel? |
| **mistake** | What is a *mistake*? What is another word that has a similar meaning? E.g. error, slip-up. |
| **lentil** | What are *lentils*? What meals do you eat that may have lentils in them? E.g. soups or stews. Have you eaten lentils? What do they taste like? |

# MOVING BEYOND THE TEXT

1. What is a fossil? How do fossils form?

2. Why do you think the beach in the story is called *Fossil Beach*? What do you think may have been found there? Do you know of other places that have a special name because of what you can see there?

3. Talk about why Mum rang Car Help even though the car only had a smashed light and it wasn't dark. Is it okay to drive a car when it is damaged?

4. What jobs sometimes need to be done to fix a car that has been in an accident? E.g. fix the dented panels, paint the damaged panels, replace broken parts.

# THE SCHWA

Gavin

family

Fossil

denim

dolphins

jacket

Robin

the

lentil

a

mistake

A

The